FUNDING YOUR VISION

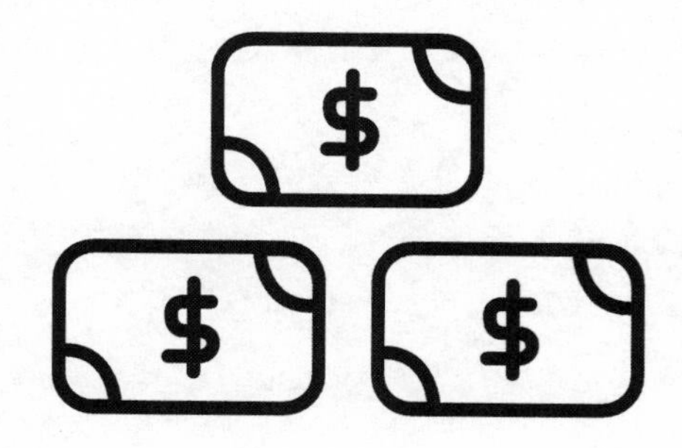

MATT ROGERS

Funding Your Vision

ISBN-10: 0-9973993-2-5

Printed in the United States of America.

CONTENTS

AN INTRODUCTION TO PASTOR'S NOTES

The gap between a seminary classroom and a pastor's desk stretches as wide as the Grand Canyon. Whether you've been to seminary, read a few books, or just burn with passion to serve God's church, it does not take long to realize that the task of pastoral ministry is more than meets the eye.

My on-ramp to pastoral ministry was convoluted to say the least. I loved Jesus and his church, and before I knew it, I was on staff in a local church. I had no clue what I was doing—a fact that was confirmed on an almost daily basis. Though I was given many opportunities to lead, I was not trained to care for God's people in the local church. I took a few seminary classes, but lacked any intentional plan to develop my theological insight or my practical ministry skills. In the years that followed, I preached sermons, taught Bible study classes, led mission trips, and organized ministry activities; however, the extent of my growth consisted of the painful process of trial and error. I'd do something that wouldn't work, so I'd do something else. I longed to be a good pastor and felt that the Spirit had given me the rudimentary skills for doing so, but I needed training. And I knew it.

A decade later, I arrived at Southeastern Baptist Theological Seminary in Wake Forest, North Carolina. There I met godly professors and fellow students who were passionate about God, his Word, and his work in the world. I learned lofty theological truths, hermeneutical paradigms, historical realities, and missiological principles that have shaped my ministry to this day. But my learning extended far beyond the seminary. In fact, my most effective training happened, not in the seats in seminary classroom, but in the day-to-day life of the local church.

By God's grace, our family joined one of a number of healthy local churches near the seminary, and there we found pastors who not only rightly communicated the glorious gospel, but also lived lives that were transformed by God's grace and gave time to training future leaders for the church. In the context of the local church, I was forced to apply the doctrine that I learned in the classroom to the real-life work of leading God's church. I found that defining a proper homiletical method is far easier than preaching a good sermon. Writing a position paper on divorce and remarriage is far easier than it is to counsel a couple experiencing the horror of a marriage on the brink of disaster. Considering the contextual realities shaping missions and evangelism in the modern world is fascinating, but those same realities become frustrating when we need to share the gospel with a neighbor or co-worker. The local church gave me a context that forced me to practice James' principle by living as a doer of the Word and not merely a hearer (Jam 1:22).

Within local church ministry, I soon learned that many of the pastor's regular activities have no guides or handbooks to help you get started. As a novice pastor, I was mesmerized by the depth of theological insight found in many of the books I was assigned. My shelves are filled with many of these works, bearing rugged spines and marked leaves to prove the impact they had on my life. Often the stated goal and broad reach of these books caused the authors to write on a macro-level. They sought to defend broad theological principles, argue for precise doctrinal claims, or establish universal definitions of the nature and mission of the church. In these books, I found a firm place for my feet to rest and step out into ministry.

Yet, I wanted and needed more. I needed books that could help me put feet to the theology they professed. I needed humble pastors who could take the "whats" and "whys" and give me some guidance on "how." I needed authors who could take the final two-sentences of application found in their chapters and tease these out into a more extensive guide for young guys like me.

That is my modest goal in *Pastor's Notes*. I write as a blue-collar theologian who loves to help pastors navigate the complexity of vocational ministry. These small books are meant to be practical guides on a host of standard pastoral issues. For this reason, they will all be incomplete. I make no effort to provide robust theological foundations, assuming that other scholars are far better equipped than me to undertake this vital task. I'll choose to build on top of the work of great thinkers and apply their insight to guide ministers in a host of practical issues ranging from teaching the church to reading the Bible, raising money, training lay leaders to provide pastoral care, developing a Constitution and Bylaws, organizing teams of lay leaders, and a host of other topics. By writing them as individual books, my intention is that these concise guides are short enough to be read in one or two sittings and are easy to read with a team of elders, deacon, staff members, or interns.

The wedding of theology and practice is vital for the health of God's church. My prayer is that these *Pastor's Notes* make a helpful contribution to enable current and future pastors to steward the glorious gift we've been entrusted—the bride of Christ—the local church.

CHAPTER ONE:

THE NEED

Money. It nags for the attention of every pastor, particularly consuming the focus of the church planter. Money is far more than a necessary evil for the church; God uses it as a vital conduit to accomplish his mission. With it, we plant churches, send missionaries, fund staffing, and run the various ministries of the church. Though we may feel a bit less-than-spiritual in admitting it, money is essential for the work to which God has called us. The goal of this short book is to aid church planters, missionaries, city mission strategists, denominational leaders, and established church pastors in raising the funds needed to fulfill their God-given vision.

THEOLOGICAL FOUNDATION

As with every other aspect of life and ministry, an effective funding strategy is predicated on several indispensable theological foundations. The goal of this book series is not to plumb the depths of these theological realities since other outstanding books like Randy Alcorn's *The Treasure Principle* spell out these truths with exceptional clarity.

At the same time, we would be foolish to take these theological foundations for granted, particularly in an area as important as money. Not only are these truths the basis of any fundraising efforts, but they also must become a steady source of hope and encouragement to any servant of the church who seeks to raise money effectively.

GOD OWNS EVERYTHING

God rightfully owns everything because he is the creator of the universe. As the Psalmist writes, "The earth is the Lord's and the fullness thereof, the world and those who dwell therein" (Ps 24:1). Everything that exists was created by him and for him (Col 1:16). When we seek to raise money, we are not trying to manufacture resources in our own power or take them back from the enemy, but trusting God to give us that which he already owns.

GOD IS SOVEREIGN OVER ALL THINGS

God is orchestrating all things for the perfect accomplishment of his mission in the world. Again, the Psalmist proclaims, "Our God is in the heavens; he does all that he pleases" (Ps 115:3). Nothing can thwart the sovereign purposes of God. Though the summit of finances may appear insurmountable, we can rest assured that God is not wringing his hands in heaven trying to figure out how to meet our needs.

GOD IS A GENEROUS GIFT-GIVER WHO LOVES TO PROVIDE FOR HIS CHILDREN

God is not a stingy Scrooge, but a good Father who loves to bless his kids. In fact, any good that you and I receive is given to us from the hand of God (Jam 1:17). God takes joy in blessing his children, the way a mother and father delight in watching their children open gifts on Christmas morning (Deut 30:9). God has already given his children the gift of salvation through Christ, yet he continues to give super-abundant gifts through his daily, ongoing provision. Fundraising is an arduous route, for sure, but we can take heart in the knowledge that God is using this work to flood our lives with his good gifts.

GOD WILL BUILD HIS CHURCH

God has promised to build his church, and he always keeps his promises (Matt 16:18). While this promise does not mean that every local church will thrive or that every church plant will succeed, it does mean that God will not fail. Such a promise should bolster our confidence that, even if don't raise enough money for our church plant, mission enterprise, or ministry venture, God has not failed. He will continue his good work of building his church—he'll just do it another way.

GOD PROVIDES FOR HIS CHURCH THROUGH THE GENEROSITY OF HIS PEOPLE

God chooses, in his wisdom, to use his people as means by which he meets the tangible needs of others. The first church was marked by such sacrificial generosity (Acts 2:44–45), and throughout the New Testament, God's people continued to give so that the message of the gospel could be proclaimed throughout the world (2 Cor 8–9).

While he could drop money from the heavens, God meets the needs of his people through the kindness of others; therefore, in our fundraising efforts, we are giving people a chance to take part in the good work he is doing throughout the world.

GOD EXPECTS HIS PEOPLE TO LIVE BY FAITH

God saves his people by faith in the finished work of Christ and empowers them to continue to live a life of faith (Rom 1:17). He longs for his people to learn to trust him as their provider, instead of depending on their own ingenuity or wisdom (Deut 8:1–10). What better gift than that of fundraising to teach us to depend on God?

Much more could be said on each of these core truths, but these simple realities build an indispensable foundation for anyone who seeks to raise money for a God-sized vision. As we raise funds for this mission, the enemy will tempt each of us to forget these truths and cower in fear. In the face of this pressure, we must return again and again to these truths, which propel our faith, expose our selfishness, and encourage us to continue to trust God and obey.

THE BENEFITS OF FULL FUNDING

Most church planters, missionaries, and pastors understand the value of money and the critical role it plays in fulfilling God's calling in their lives. Yet, they often treat fundraising as little more than a necessary evil before they can move on to the work that is seemingly more important.

As a result, typical fundraisers bolt out of the starting blocks with passion and energy. The first leg of the race often goes well, characterized by God's provision; however, after this surge, the going gets tough. They meet some obstacles. They grow tired. And then, they begin to rationalize the need to move on to more important responsibilities:

- "What's a little debt, at least we've got some money in the bank. Plus, if we wait to build this new building, it's going to be too late, and we are going to start loosing people."
- "God's called me to plant a church. I know I've only raised enough money to make it for a couple of months, and our family has no money in savings, but we've got to get after it. We've got a core team in place and a city in need of the gospel. I can't sit around and spend any more time raising money."
- "We've been poor before. I'll empty out my retirement money and pick up a second or third job. Surely if we scramble for a year or two, we will have a tithe base to support a full-time pastor."
- "I'll just figure it out as we go along. I've been waiting for years to be overseas sharing the gospel, and nothing is going to stop me now."

Our excuses are endless, demonstrating how easy it is to downplay proper funding for God's calling. The difference between having twenty percent of the needed funds and having 100 percent is stark. Consider a few of the results that come from being fully funded.

YOU ARE FREE FROM WORRYING ABOUT MONEY

Financial stress muddies our thinking and consumes our thoughts. Unless you are a rare individual with massive brain space to spare, you will find yourself limited in what you can attend to at any one time. In the context of a church plant, we have much to attend to once we start staff meetings, small groups, sermon preparation, counseling, and mission projects. Those who lack full funding have the incessant sound of fundraising hovering overhead, demanding attention or worry. Often, due to the demands of day-to-day ministry, this mental margin is relegated to the hours we spend tossing and turning in our beds trying to fall asleep or to the time we should be praying for the needs of others.

YOUR FAMILY IS FREE FROM THE BURDEN OF INSUFFICIENT FINANCES

If you have a family, rest assured that your financial stresses are not limited to you alone. The whole family feels the strain of bills that need to be paid or necessary expenses that have been deferred. The wear-and-tear of finances on a family can lead to untold strain on marriages and children, who invariably experience the secondhand stress that money often brings. Full funding is not meant to allow a family to live in luxury or match the standard of living of their peers, but it should free them from having to wonder whether or not they will get their next meal.

YOU ARE FREE TO FOCUS FULLY ON THE MISSION

Full funding propels missionaries, church planters, or pastors on the mission God has birthed in their heart. Every person has a limited capacity. Let's assume that a person lacks full funding, and in turn, allocates 80% of their capacity to the work God has called them to and another 20% to fundraising. The exchange may appear helpful over the short run, but compounded over several months, the 20% of time adds up. The allotted 20% of time represents counseling sessions you can't do, sermons preparation that you must neglect, mission in which you cannot engage, and a host of other meaningful work that goes undone. Imagine the effectiveness of a missionary who devoted six months of 100% intentionality to the work of fundraising and was then free to devote 100% of their time to the work of international missions for the rest of their lives.

YOU ARE PROTECTED FROM THE TEMPTATION TO GROW FOR THE WRONG REASONS

Church planters are particularly susceptible to the temptation to force their congregations to grow quickly so they can establish a tithing base. The lure of quick growth may cause these pastors to hastily move up the launch of a Sunday service or shy away from hard conversations with potential church members. They may drive home on Sunday afternoons thinking, "I wonder how much people gave today?" instead of asking, "I wonder if we are taking the proper steps in planting this church?" Most church planters discover that who *does not* stay in the early days of the church is just as important as who *does* stay. Full funding gives those who stay a pastor with the freedom to run off wolves without worrying about the implications on the tithing base of the church.

YOU ARE ABLE TO ADD OTHER PEOPLE TO YOUR TEAM

Plural leadership is vital for healthy church planting and mission work because omni-compotent individuals don't exist. Church leaders who are self-aware will recognize holes in their giftedness and call on others to fill these gaps. Yet, insufficient funding makes it all-but-impossible to add others to our team. Who in their right mind would want to join a team when those who are already on the team are constantly scrambling to provide the needed funds for their families? No one. But, when our needs are met, we can clearly, compellingly, and realistically invite others to join with us in God's mission. Only if we have been successful in raising money are we positioned to help others on our team to do it as well.

YOU HAVE THE TANGIBLE EVIDENCE OF THE FAITHFULNESS OF GOD

Finally, full funding places a constant reminder of the faithfulness of God in front of you on a daily basis. Like the nation of Israel, you will be able to sing songs of God's kindness for the rest of your life. I still remember sitting in Panera Bread and opening an envelope from a potential donor. In it was a pledge card that pushed us over the threshold of the money we needed to plant our first church. As my eyes filled with tears, I was overwhelmed by God's goodness. This is a memory I'll never forget, and reflecting on that moment propelled me to trust God during many days of self-doubt and discouragement.

The theological and practical basis for fundraising should motivate you to embark on this journey. Yet, mere exuberance is not enough. We must have a plan.

GO TO THE ANT

Solomon, the wise king of Israel, exhorted those who desire wisdom to watch an ant. He writes, "Go to the ant, O sluggard; consider her ways, and be wise. Without having any chief, officer, or ruler, she prepares her bread in summer and gathers her food in harvest" (Proverbs 6:6–8). Ants have a plan. They work when others sleep. They execute a strategy and reap a harvest for their labors.

Similar to an ant, God's people pray and plan. Certainly God blesses us in ways we'd never imagine and apart from any intentionality on our part on occasion. In addition, God often changes our plans to show that he has a better path for us. These truths are not meant to lull us into passivity. They are meant to give us confidence to make a plan and seek to execute that plan, knowing that God is at work at all times to shape the trajectory of our actions and move them into conformity with his good purposes. So, perhaps a good question is: how would an ant raise money?

CHAPTER TWO:

THE STRATEGY

There is no shortage of quick-fix methods for fundraising, but these "weight loss pill" fundraising strategies are prone to over-promise and under-deliver. You could launch a GoFundMe account or blitz social media with your financial needs. Alternatively, you could do what most people do when they want to raise money—send fund-raising letters.

Here's how fundraising normally works. You are going on a mission trip to Bangladesh and need to raise $5,000 to make this trip happen. You rush to cobble together a list of family and friends who might be interested in your mission. If your experience matches that of many church planters, you have a small circle of people who would fund anything you put your mind to—from starting an elephant farm to launching a clothing line for adolescent hipsters. You pound out a quick letter explaining the nature of your mission and requesting the needed money and send it to this select group with a return envelope for them to return to you with a check. Over time, most of the money rolls in. If you fall a bit short, you always have your parents, local church, or ministry leaders to make up the difference.

This method may work to get you to Bangladesh on a short-term missions trip, but such a haphazard approach is unlikely to produce the funds needed to plant a church over the next two or three years. And, if you try these types of strategies first, you are likely to undermine the success that a better plan could produce. Typical of effective plans, fundraising will require an intentional strategy and much more effort to result in long-term success. Let's think of a good fundraising strategy in four successive stages.

THE STRATEGY

Long before letters are written or meetings are held, those who raise funds effectively develop a strategy. The first item on this strategy list is to establish a realistic fundraising budget to accomplish God's mission.

BUILD A STRATEGY FOR MONEY

Each ministry context demands a uniquely contextualized fundraising plan. The amount required for a family of six to plant a church in urban Los Angeles differs widely from the funding needed for a single female to serve in an orphanage in a third-world country upon graduation from college. While budgeting down to the last penny you'll need for the next 3 years is an impossible feat, drafting a baseline budget is feasible for any location.

The best place to start when developing a funding number is to ask people who have done it recently. In most cities throughout the United States, you will be able to find another church planter or local pastor who can give you their cost of living and start-up costs that may be normative in that location. Area denominational leaders can also help discern a needed funding goal. If you are going to work with an existing church or mission, then that ministry should be able to send you a well-defined funding goal. But if all else fails, you can still determine this goal without these resources and contacts. Simply asking patrons at a local coffee shop a series of questions will help you assess the expected cost of living. After all, you don't have to be a pastor to know how much it costs to rent a place to live, buy groceries, and pay your bills.

This funding goal should not only include the amount needed to fund the personal expense of the pastor or missionary, but also any costs needed to accomplish the leader's vision. For example, a church planter should also consider a budget for renting a space to gather on Sundays or the price of equipment for audio-visual needs or children's ministry.

In addition, you must calculate how long you expect to need outside funding. For some, the plan is to depend on outside support for the entirety of their mission work. Ministries such as Campus Crusade for Christ, have based their ministry on such a model. Those who work for Cru will always depend on outside support and will never be on the payroll of the ministry itself. For most, lifelong support is not the goal. Church planters will often design their strategy with the assumption that, at a certain time, the church itself will be able to support their pastor's salary and budgetary needs. This timeline, similar to the funding need itself, depends on many contextual factors. The time to develop a self-supporting ministry to urban teenagers in a poverty-stricken inner-city location is wildly different from how long it will take to plant a church in suburban

Atlanta. Again, fellow ministry leaders in the city can help you project a reasonable timeline.

A word of warning is necessary at this point. Always overestimate both the amount of money you need and the length of time you will need it. Telling donors that you no longer need their support is far easier than going back to them and asking for more. In addition, raising more money two years into a church plant is much more difficult than raising enough for three years before launching the plant.

If you are married, you must avoid working in isolation and, instead, make the funding goal a team project. Church planters are notorious for cutting corners and short-changing their family in the process. Make sure that your spouse helps set the funding number and is comfortable that the budget is enough to support the needs of the family.

Upon completion of this first step in the funding strategy process, you should be able to write down the exact financial budget and length of time for which you are seeking funding. You should be able to say, with clarity, that you are raising $150,000 for three years to plant a church in New York. An overseas missionary may determine that they will need $40,000 to work among an unreached people group for one year.

Often you will hear planters or missionaries articulate a tiered goal, such as $180,000 for year 1, $120,000 for year 2, and $40,000 for year 3. This strategy seems clear: the continued development of the church should allow for the tithing based on the congregation to carry an increasing portion of the financial burden. In year 1, the planter and the church will be entirely dependent on outside support; by year two, the church can fund 30% of the work; by year 3, it can sustain 60%, and so on. This principle is *always* the reality in practice, but you should *rarely* articulate this in the public fundraising strategy. When casting vision, telling potential donors that you need differing amounts for differing years is cumbersome and confusing. In most cases, you should communicate a fixed need for a determined timespan. Then, as your church becomes self-supporting, you will be able to sustain those who fail to keep their giving commitment or go back to donors and tell them that their giving is no longer needed and that they can now give to support another ministry.

Once you have this number in place, it's helpful in communicating vision to break this support goal into bite-sized chunks. Some fundraising strategists argue that you should work to secure only big donors; however, this approach is fraught with difficulties. While a rare and fortunate individual may find Mr. and Mrs. Moneybags who can write a single check that will underwrite the entire ministry, this is far from the norm. Most fundraisers will find their needs met through an army of donors who give in smaller increments. By overtly stating this as a goal, you will encourage people who want to give to your work, but feel that they lack the resources to give a large sum. I would suggest that you break your funding goal into three tiers: $100 per month, $50 per month, and $25 per month (more will be said regarding monthly giving versus onetime giving later in this book).

Tiered giving normalizes the need of your ministry. When people hear that you need $120,000, they are prone to assume that you are asking them to write a check for $10 grand. But, when you say that you need $50 per month, many more people will feel that they can be involved in your work. Also, though the $100 level is unlikely to inspire as many donors, it produces a high-end anchor to the giving and will cause many to choose the middle level. For example, if you walk into Target to buy a coffee pot and see three models priced at $25, $50, and $100, most buyers will purchase the $50 version, assuming that the $25 model is cheap and fragile, and the $100 model is designed for the elite.

Smaller levels of giving mobilize more people to be involved in your work. If you have two donors supporting your entire ministry, then those two are likely to be engaged in prayer and partnership as well. If you have two hundred donors giving to your ministry, then you have a massive army of people engaged in other ways as well. Finally, smaller levels of partnership protects the planter or missionary from feeling the crushing loss that comes when a big donor stops giving. If you have two donors giving $20,000 annually, then you notice when one of them stops giving. If you have two hundred donors giving $25 a month, then you can sustain the burden when life circumstances cause a few of them to fall away.

Then organize the giving categories into the number of givers needed at each level. Put approximately 50% of the people in the lowest level ($25 per month), 35% in the second level ($50 per month), and 15% in the highest level ($100 per month). Here's an example:

With this precisely defined goal and financial breakdown in place, you are well on your way to meeting with potential donors and securing the needed funding for your work.

BUILD A STRATEGY FOR PEOPLE

The second step in the strategy phase is to build a plan for potential donors. Let's assume you need 200 givers based on your fundraising number. Now you have to figure out where you are going to find that many people to be involved in your work.

Excel becomes your best friend at this stage. Whether you like it or not, strategies need organization, and the spreadsheets you create at this stage will be a great asset to you further down the road (a sample spreadsheet is available for download at *mattrogers.bio/funding*). Begin to brainstorm a list of donors and put their names in alphabetical order in the first column of your spreadsheet.

Begin with the names of individual donors. Resist the urge to talk yourself out of contacting people that you think will not give. Be forewarned that some of those you assume will give will not give you a penny, and some of those you assume will not give will become your best supporters.

So, just begin to make a list of names. You may find it helpful to think through various categories of people as you brainstorm this list. Start with the easiest group—the people you are around most often at this time in your life—to build momentum toward reaching your goal. This first group will likely involve people from your church, work, or neighborhood who already know that God is stirring in your heart and are predisposed to give. Also, include immediate family members at this first stage of brainstorming as they will often be the first to contribute to your work.

Second, think through the main locations in which you and your spouse have lived through the years. Stop at each season of life and brainstorm those with whom you had a close relationship at that time. This process might look something like this:

Home church where you grew up	
High School Friends	
College	

The Wonder Years (aka that two-year stretch of aimlessness when you were trying to "find yourself")	
First three years of marriage in rural Georgia	
Full-time associate pastor at First Baptist Church	

Third, think back through your life in terms of the types of people that you know. Here are general categories of the types of people that fall on most people's fundraising list. Beside each heading, think of a couple of specific names of people who have played that role in your life.

Spiritual mentors	
Pastors or Bible Study leaders	

Close family friends	
Current or Former Co-workers	
Current or Former Neighbors	
Workers you see often (dentist, doctor, barista, waitress, etc.)	
Those with whom you share hobbies (bikers, hunters, runners, etc.)	
Those who have done what you are about to do already (people who planted a church five years ago, were missionaries in the 70's, etc.)	

People who have a unique passion for the work you are doing (those who lived in the city in which you are planting or who were born in the location of your mission work)	
People who are known as benefactors of faith-based work in your city	

You may think of more categories to add on your own, but this list should give you a good start.

Finally, add the names of various groups of people to this list. We will examine these groups later, but there may be occasions when approaching an entire group of people is better than meeting with isolated individuals. This might include a local church, a denominational group, a Sunday School class, or small group. There may be overlap between some of the names of those on your individual's list and those who show up on this list. For example, you may list a name of a family friend who happens to be in a Sunday School class that your parents attend. By listing the group as well, you tap into an outer-concentric circle of relationships that you might not approach in a one-on-one fashion. If you speak to this Sunday School class, you will cast vision in front of your family friend, but you'll also be able to share in front of five or six other couples who you never would have been able to tell about your vision for the church plant or mission work.

In order to develop this list effectively, you are going to need help from at least two sources. First, ask someone to help you who has walked through much of life by your side. For many, this will be a spouse who knows many of the same people and was with you at many of these life stages. Take time on one of those boring drives to visit grandparents and think through this list. You will be surprised at how many more names will surface when you brainstorm together. Use your parents as you prepare your lists. Again, they know many of the same people and have walked with you through all of life, so they have a good bit to offer. Tell them what you are doing and ask if they could create a similar list and then compare notes. They will come in handy for names of those from your home church, extended family, friends, or known benefactors in their local church.

Second, use every database at your disposal in order to build this list. Think about the various places where you have names listed or stored, such as a Christmas card mailing list, your wedding directory, or your cell phone. Comb through those lists and pull out names as you go. Another great tool for adding to your database is social media. While you may not really be "friends" with many of the people on your "friend list," you can leverage those names to populate your list.

Remember, avoid the urge to talk yourself out of adding people and go ahead and place their name to the list. What's the worst that could happen? The random high school buddy you haven't spoken to in twenty years ignores you. Who cares? Do not feel compelled to limit this list to believers or those who understand the necessity of missions and church planting. One aspect of the common grace of God is that many non-believers still give to charitable causes on a regular basis. If they are going to give to an organization, why not ask them to give to you?

One last question is vital before we move on: What is a goal for the number of names you need on your list? Typically, you will need twice as many names on your list as the number of funding supporters you need to meet you goal. If your funding goal looks like this:

Total Goal: $120,000 for three years

Plan: 30 people giving $100 per month = $36,000

75 people giving $50 per month = $45,000

130 people giving $25 per month = $39,000

According to your plan, and some outstanding middle school math, you will need 235 donors to reach this goal. We've found that those who use a plan like the one outlined in this book will have about 50% of those on their list give to their work; therefore, your original list needs to have twice as many names as you donor needs—in this case, you'd need 470 names. You can see why brainstorming is so vital. You aren't likely to raise enough money to plant a church by asking your twelve best buddies. It's going to take more work than that.

BUILD A STRATEGY FOR TIME

Little needs to be said about this part of the strategy phase, but success is impossible without it. In order to raise money well, you are going to have to treat this work like a full-time job. You will not raise money effectively in your spare time. Yet, fundraising is hard work, and you will naturally drift towards passivity unless you force yourself to make it a top priority. Before you begin, you must figure out how you will restructure your life in order to raise funds well.

This will mean assessing your finances to decide how much freedom you may have to raise funds. It may mean moving from full-time to part-time at your company. It may mean stepping away from your full-time ministry in the church. It may mean doing what we did, moving your stuff into storage and living with your in-laws for a summer to devote full-time energy to fundraising. You likely have many objections in your mind at this point in the process. But, before you excuse yourself out of this step because, well, you just have to have a full-time job, please consider the priority of this work. If you devote 10 percent energy to fundraising, you will get limited results and be forced to continue to raise money indefinitely. Remember the theological principles we established at the outset of the book and prayerfully and creatively develop a plan that will allow you to devote the greatest amount of time possible to raising money.

Vigorously resist the temptation to launch your church plant or missionary work too quickly. If you do so, you will only add a responsibility to your plate that will, like a snowball, inevitably grow in the time it consumes as you delay securing necessary funding. Far too many church planters assume that they can launch a few small groups, host preview services, and begin staff meetings while they are raising money. This laudable goal will soon become a liability. Small groups mean people, and people mean problems—broken marriages, addictions, and faulty relationships—all of which are difficulties that you, as their pastor, must address. Preview services require sermon preparation and the planning of the creative elements that are involved in corporate worship. Everyone is limited—limited in terms of our time and the mental margin we have to devote to a set number of tasks. If this space is filled with a host of necessary responsibilities for your mission work, then you may end up crowding out time for fundraising.

BUILD A STRATEGY FOR YOUR COMMUNICATION

Your first step in communication with potential donors will come in the form of an **introductory letter**; however, the model espoused in this book ultimately relies upon face-to-face, eye-to-eye contact with those whom you ask for money. This first letter is not meant to be a fundraising letter per se but a means to establishing contact to request a personal meeting. The letter should introduce yourself and your family, give the reader a sense of what God is doing in your life, describe the challenges you face, discuss your plan of action, and conclude with an invitation for a meeting. Thus, the general outline of the letter is something like this:

I. Introduction
II. Calling
III. Challenges
IV. Plan
V. Request

Here is the letter my family used to raise funds to plant Renewal Church in Greenville, South Carolina in the summer of 2009.

Dear Friend,
I hear the same story from different people almost every day. It goes something like this:

"I grew up in the South, where everybody calls themselves Christians. I even when to church and was an active member of my youth group growing up. I thought I knew what it meant to be a Christian, but I was wrong. Now I just do my own thing—I gave up on God and the church a long time ago."

What makes this story compelling is that it was my story. I, too, grew up in a Christian family, went to church, and missed Jesus. But God, in his grace, continued to pursue me with his love and captivate me with his kindness. I trusted in Jesus' work and have committed to giving my life away to serve his church.

Our shared passion for God's church has compelled Sarah and me to prayerfully and intentionally take steps toward establishing a new church in the upstate of South Carolina. God has sealed his calling in our lives over the last year, and we are committed to planting Renewal Church in 2009. Our desire is that people from all walks of life will have a chance to experience the life offered through the gospel of Jesus Christ.

This vision has been confirmed by our current pastors, seminary faculty, and other denominational leaders. The challenging is daunting. Currently in Greenville County only 16.2% of the population of half a million people profess to have a relationship with Jesus Christ and a connection to the local church. That means that, in the heart of the Bible Belt, there are approximately 400,000 people without saving faith. We want to do something about that.

We are excited about seeing what God will do through our work. Our plan is to move to Mauldin, South Carolina at the end of the summer to begin our work. In the meantime, we are seeking to connect with as many people as possible who may be interested in partnering with us in this work. I plan to call you over the next few weeks to see about setting up a time when we can meet and talk more about this new church plant and how you can help us move forward. Until then, you can learn more about our church online at www.renewalupstate.com. I look forward to seeing you soon.

Blessings,
Matt, Sarah, Corrie, and Avery Rogers

Writing this letter is the first step in your communication plan. More will be said about how to use it in the next stage. For now, note a few key details. First, the letter does not contain any request for money, nor does it include a self-addressed envelope for them to put a check and mail back to you. As stated earlier, such an approach is far simpler, but will yield far less results. You can easily raise $3,000 to go to Africa using that approach, but you will rarely be able to raise $120,000 for three years that way. Second, the letter is brief. Make sure it fits on one page and is clear and concise. Finally, notice that the letter has a clear next step—you intend to call them in the coming days to set up a time to meet. Craft your letter, get someone to proofread it, and file it away for now.

Second, you are going to need a **vision document** that clearly and compellingly states your vision for the new work. The document needs to be a single-page, front and back, full color presentation of the critical information about your vision. On the front side, you should include the basic newspaper information (who, what, when, where, and why), and on the reverse, include the ways that others can be involved. The vision document we used for the same church plant is available as a free download at: *mattrogers.bio/funding*.

A third part of your communication plan should be a **follow up post-card**. On one side, include space for the basic contact information from the donor, and on the back, include the various ways that they might agree to take part in your work. The ways they can be involved should follow the layout of the headers from the back page of your vision document. This will be the card you use to collect information and track your donor base (a really big deal).

Finally, you will likely want to establish an **online presence**. Your website can include more information than is found on your vision document, and it will serve as a primary way people learn more about the work you are doing. At this point, you do not need a complex site—a simple Wordpress, Wix, or SquareSpace site will do (some donation-centric web tools like GivingFuel may also fit the bill). In fact, an overly complex site will work against you. Simply include the basic information from your vision document, though in greater detail, videos and pictures of your missionary context or your team, a statement of faith, and a portal through which donors can give to your work online. Many donor portals are specifically designed to facilitate online giving (our church uses eGiving, but others such as EasyTithe, SimpleGive, and Tithe.ly provide comparable pricing and services), and you would be wise to set one up from the outset. This will allow donors to schedule regular giving to your church each month and make life far more stress-free for you since you will not have to depend on people to mail their checks each month.

Some people may see fit to draft a full church-planting prospectus, a multi-page document describing the vision and mission of the work in more detail. I would *encourage* you to develop such a document, but I would *discourage* you from using it in most of your fundraising. The average donor will grow restless with too much information—particularly information that could just as easily live online. Those who may want a full-blown prospectus are likely to be pastors, deacon boards, or denominational leaders. You will be well-served to have such a document for these relationships, but you will not need it for most of your private donors. Space does not allow for a full prospectus to be included in this *Pastor's Notes*, but you can easily take the main categories of your vision document and expand them into full-page descriptions, craft some charts, graphs, and visuals, and include your statement of faith. *Viola*! You have a prospectus. If you need further direction on creating your prospectus, I've written a guide that's available here: http://sendnetwork.com/2015/03/09/writing-a-church-planting-prospectus/

In total, you should have at least four main pieces with which to communicate your vision. Make sure you take care to design these tools with quality and excellence and avoid cutting corners. Let someone else see them and give you feedback. Once you have them in final form, then you are ready to execute your fundraising plan.

CHAPTER THREE:

THE MEETING

The second stage begins when you mail the introductory letter. Do not—and I repeat: *do not*—mail all the letters at one time. Remember, the letter ends by saying that you plan to call them to set up a time when you can meet. So, only mail the number of letters that you can reasonably follow up with over the course of a week. The maximum number you will be able to connect with will likely be around 20 letters per week.

Mail letters in strategic geographies so that you can meet with all the people in a certain location before moving on to another geographical region. If, for example, you have people on your list in South Carolina, Kentucky, and Georgia, you should not mail the letters to all three states at the same time. Rather, mail the letters to those in South Carolina, and then go to South Carolina to meet with those individuals. Then, mail the letters to those in Kentucky, go to Kentucky to have those meetings, and so on.

Once you mail the letters, wait about three days and begin to make phone calls to that list of people. If you mail the letters on Monday, you should be able to make all twenty calls on Wednesday. Making these calls will likely be your most intimidating task. You can expect roughly 50–60% of the people you call to be willing to meet with you. Yes, that number is correct. Recall that I said approximately 50% of those on your original brainstorm list will fund your work, and this same percentage of people will be willing to meet with you. This means that nearly everyone who is willing to meet will give to your work in some way. The downside of this reality is that you will learn who these 50% are during these phone calls. Some of the people will simply ignore you. They won't answer your call and won't call you back. Others will take your call and continually make veiled excuses as to why they cannot meet. A select few will tell you clearly that they have no interest in meeting with you or hearing about your work. Be prepared to fight discouragement during this stage.

The upside is that most of the painful conversations will happen on the phone. Those who are willing to meet with you are likely to know that you will be asking them for money and have already considered how they plan to give. Their willingness to schedule a meeting with you is a sign of their support for your work.

If you are like me, making phone calls is one of your least favorite things to do. I'd prefer to send a quick text message or even a group text (oh, the horror)! You must fight to urge to take the easy way out. While texts and emails are far easier and deflect the rejection you may face if you actually have to talk to someone, they seem impersonal and are easily ignored. Just think of how many messages you delete or ignore on a daily basis. They have become the modern day form of junk mail. Phone calls, on the other hand, allow someone to hear the passion in your voice and connect with the story God is writing with your life. They allow you the ability to connect with your potential donors in a personal way and begin the work of inviting them to join you in your mission. So, fight the urge to be lazy and give your thumbs a break—pick up the phone and make the call.

What you need to say during the phone call is simple. After you greet them, you should ask if they received the letter you sent in the mail. Be prepared for many to say they did not. Perhaps the wife opened the mail, yet the husband answers the call or visa versa. Maybe the mail is thrown in a basket and only sorted once a week. In either case, you need to be prepared to explain why you are calling to the person who answers the call. This should be a simple, quick recap of what they would have read had they received the letter. Then ask if there would be a good time to meet up with them in the next week.

Again, you need to have a blank schedule so you can plan meetings at a time that is convenient for them. Suggest getting coffee or lunch at some point during the week, or even inviting them over for dinner at your home one night. Seek to schedule your most unlikely time slots first. For example, don't schedule a widow for a meeting at lunch on Tuesday—a time when most businessmen may be free to meet. Ask if you can come by the widow's home on Wednesday morning at 10:00 am when few people can meet and keep the prime slots open. As you call, don't forget to record the exact time and location of the meeting on your calendar. There is nothing worse than scheduling a meeting for 10:00 am at Atlanta Bread Company, yet showing up at Panera at 10:30 am. Continue to use the Excel spreadsheet in which you brainstormed names of donors and simply add columns to track your progress through the fundraising journey.

Beside their name and contact information, create a column for sending the introductory letter, another for making the phone call, and another for scheduling a meeting. This document will become a one-stop-shop for all of your administrative tasks. A sample spreadsheet is available at mattrogers.bio/funding.

When the day of the meeting arrives, prepare for each meeting with prayer, entrusting your efforts to the guidance of God's Spirit. After all, he is the one doing the real work. Dress appropriately for your funding appointments. My go-to rule of thumb is always dress one level above the expected dress of the person with whom you are meeting. So, if you are meeting with a college student, jeans and polo shirt would be fine. If you are meeting a family friend, then business casual is likely best. If you are meeting with a business professional, then you might want to throw on a tie or a nice dress. Do not underestimate the significance of these types of decisions. The professionalism with which you carry yourself and communicate your vision will go a long way to determining the nature of the support you receive. This is human nature—we all want to give our money to those who take their work seriously and have thought through the details of their venture—whether we are investing in a start up company or a local orphanage.

Second, you must be on time. In fact, you should plan to be at the location of your meeting at least five minutes ahead of schedule and be there when your appointment arrives. Once they arrive and the conversation begins, honor their time. Do not ramble about secondary matters for 30 minutes of a 45-minute meeting.

Begin by asking questions—particularly if you are meeting with someone you have not seen in a long time. Ask about their job, their family, and, if they are a believer, their local church. If appropriate, you might ask them to tell you what God has been doing in their life lately.

Their current leading sets up a natural transition for you to share what God has been doing in your life. Share your story in brief and transition to describing the work to which God is calling you and your family. Allow the first page of your vision document to guide this part of the discussion. Describe your vision for the work, the location, your plan, and the team with whom you will be working. In closing, describe the unique challenges of the work you will be doing and some of the major needs you face.

CHAPTER FOUR:

THE ASK

As one of my seminary professors used to say, "Now it's time to put your big boy pants on." The "ask" is the third stage in successful fund-raising. After describing your mission using the front side of the vision document, turn the page to present three primary ways others can be involved in your work. Don't feel the need to shy away from a bold, crisp, and compelling request at this point. Those whom you meet with already know that you are going to ask for their help. So, avoid the middle-school dance syndrome and ask the individual to dance!

The first area to ask people to be involved is praying for your work. This is a vital need and a way that all people can be involved in your work. Avoid the temptation to run straight to a financial request or to discount those who state that they will commit to pray for your ministry. Compile those names just as you do with those who give financially, building a prayer list through which you can communicate critical needs to this insider team of prayer warriors.

Then, ask them to consider giving to your work. Remember most people have no idea what is normal, so use your three categories of givers to explain how people can be involved in your work. Ask them to consider supporting you with a monthly donation at one of these levels. Prioritize asking people to give on a monthly basis rather than simply writing a one-time check.

Monthly giving has many advantages over one-time giving. First, most monthly givers remain invested for the long haul. If they are writing a check each month—even a small check for $25—they are more likely to pray for your work and seek out ways to continue to be involved. Second, most monthly givers end up contributing more in the end. It feels like a great gift to receive a check for $250 (and it is), but you are far better off in the long run if someone agrees to give you $25 a month over three years. Finally, monthly givers provide a steady stream of ongoing support. Since most people are unlikely to be self-supporting missionaries or church planters until two years into their work, you would be well served to have funding that will last until that time, rather than having an inflated bank account at the outset that you watch dwindle each month until you run out of money.

Feel free to share with potential donors the budget you have left to raise and stories of those who have already given. I vividly recall a young college guy who agreed to support our church plant at $25 a month because "that was little more than the cost of a nice dinner out." Throughout our fundraising journey, I used his story to show that anybody could give something to meet our funding needs.

Besides just asking for monetary support, you may see fit to ask them to consider giving tangible items that you will need. For example, some business professionals may be able to donate computers or sound equipment, or some families may be able to give children's toys or cribs.

Finally, ask people to be involved in your work. This may mean referring you to other people who might be interested in supporting you. For example, if you've exhausted all of your contacts and still have a shortage of people on your brainstorm list, then you may need to leverage the relationships of others to extend your pool of contacts. You might ask, "Do you know anyone else who might be interested in being involved in the work we are doing?" Or, if you are planting a church near the donor's home, you might ask them to refer friends to you who need a healthy church. Don't forget to ask them to consider being involved in short-term or long-term mission work alongside of you. You may be surprised when someone does more than simply give you money, but feels led to uproot their life and move with you to help your vision become a reality.

Refer the potential donor to the commitment card and ask them to commit to their giving in print and return the card to you. Many times individuals will need additional time to consider their level of giving following the meeting. For example, if a person meets with you without his or her spouse, then they will likely need time to talk with their spouse before making any commitment. Encourage them to take the card and drop it in the mail to you sometime over the following week once they've solidified their commitment.

Either way it is vital that you explain the mechanisms of giving to the donor. First, ask if they would be willing to schedule their giving online. Some will be willing to do so while others may be squeamish about giving in this way. Explain the benefits to you of online giving and ask the donor to consider this route first. Ideally, you can show them the online portal for giving through your church's website and go ahead and set up their account. Those who wish to give by writing a check should be given the name and mailing address of the church and encouraged that their gifts are tax deductible. The church mailing address should be on the vision document that you will leave with them. Be aware that people are unlikely to remember to send in a check at the first of each month. Most successful fundraisers will write a monthly newsletter to all of their donors and include a self-addressed envelope for their donor base to enclose their monthly giving.

CHAPTER FIVE:

THE FOLLOW-THROUGH

The first, and I do mean first, action step after meeting with a donor is to record their giving on your Excel document. Most people will have no problem remembering to record a commitment from a donor who pledges to give $250 each month; however, you may forget that Mr. and Mrs. Robinson asked to have time to pray over their decision and promised to return their card later in the week. Take time to make a notation of the response of each individual with whom you meet and develop a plan to circle back to those who need time before giving you an answer.

How long should you give people to consider how they will contribute to your work? There is no magic number, but the reality is that most people do not need extended time to make this decision. They likely need the time to go home, talk it over with their spouse, look at their budget, and spend some time in prayer. The modern pace of life may mean that they can't do all of this on the same day you meet with them. But, they do not need one month to do this either. Typically, you should err on the side of caution and give potential donors approximately one week before you follow up.

Once again, I would recommend that you follow up with a phone call rather than via text message or email, which can seem aggressive or pushy. Simply call those with whom you've met and ask if they've had time to think about supporting your work. Some people may use this intervening time to go AWOL. It is not likely, but a few of your potential donors may disappear by simply avoiding your calls. After you've attempted to contact them three times, assume they do not want to give and move on. Some people may tell you that they need more time. Again, it is not likely, but if they do, simply ask when you should call back and note this in your spreadsheet. Most people who've had one week to consider support will be ready to give you an answer at that time. When they do, thank them for their support, and write down the nature of that support (prayer, giving, or partnership) in your Excel document.

The second action step is to send a thank you note to all those who agree to support your work. Notice that I did not say, send them a thank you email or text message. Again, the greater the personalization the better. In a culture where handwritten notes are rare, it demonstrates care and thoughtfulness when you write a handwritten note of thanks to your donors. Get in the habit of writing these letters at the same time as you enter the giving amount in your spreadsheet. Let your thankfulness for God's provision overflow in thankfulness to your donors.

Following up also involves writing a monthly newsletter to update your donors on the progress of the mission. Stories of your work are the most powerful way to accomplish this goal. Most donors do not want lists of objectives or details of ministry philosophy.

They want to read stories of changed lives. A self-addressed giving envelope should be enclosed in each of these monthly newsletters. For an example of one such letter from The Church at Greer Station, a church that we were able to help plant using a similar funding strategy in 2014, visit mattrogers.bio/funding.

You can also create a simple e-newsletter, perhaps using MailChimp, with the same content and a link to online giving. But, you should not send an e-news update without also sending a print version. For one thing, the print version is a far better cue to most people that they should give. Second, some people—such as most senior adults or blue-collar workers—do not have email access, or do not check it often. Finally, electronic correspondence is easy to discard in the piles of spam mail most receive. You may see fit to ask your donors if they'd prefer a print or electronic version so that you avoid wasting postage on those who prefer an e-news update.

Finally, follow through requires that you track your donors' giving. This responsibility is best streamlined using the Excel document you've created throughout your fundraising work. You can create columns for each month and track the giving as it is received. Be patient if you notice that someone has not contributed. Some may have forgotten or been negligent while others may be planning to give on a bi-monthly or quarterly basis. If you notice that someone has not given for three consecutive months without telling you why, then you should call and check-in with him or her. Remember, you are not a bill collector. You are a missionary, a church planter, or a pastor. First, check on the donor to make sure they haven't experienced a job loss or some other life-altering catastrophe. Second, check to make sure they know how to give and are receiving your monthly newsletter. Particularly if they are giving to you for the first time, there may be a myriad of practical reasons they've been unable to give, even if they are willing to do so. Finally, check on their giving frequency. Ask if they plan to give on a monthly, quarterly, or yearly basis. These three questions will give your donors the space to share their difficulties without you assuming the posture of a bill collector.

CHAPTER SIX:

THE QUESTIONS

BUT, WHAT ABOUT...?

Most readers will naturally have additional questions about the plan outlined above. Human nature quickly poses all sorts of "but, what about" questions to the plan outlined above. No fundraising model will ever be able to tackle every aspect of the complexity of funding your ministry needs. The model above is meant to construct the scaffolding for you to then build an effective plan to raise the money you need to fund God's vision in your life. Here are a few common "but, what about...?" questions that I often hear.

BUT, WHAT ABOUT PEOPLE WHO LIVE TOO FAR AWAY?

Don't be surprised if see a good number of people on your original brainstorm list who live in hard to visit locales. We all have relational connections—family and friends—scattered all over the world. This will particularly be true if you've moved often throughout your life or live a long way from the town in which you grew up.

The process can, and should, follow a similar pattern, even for those you can't see personally. You should still send your introductory letter and make the first phone call; however, in that call you do not ask for a time to meet face-to-face but rather a time to Skype or meet via a Google Hangout (or whatever other technological platform strikes your fancy). Video is critical here. Rather than attempting to do the fundraising appointment via a phone call, seek to carve out time when you can meet with them on video and walk through your funding presentation just as if you were meeting with them in person.

BUT, WHAT ABOUT MY FAMILY?

It is wise to involve the entire family in the fundraising journey. In fact, many of the donors on your original list are likely to be primarily connected to one or the other of you. For example, your wife's best friend from college and her family or your husband's co-worker may make the list. These meetings require that both the husband and wife attend the meeting.

But, as anyone with children knows, getting the kids ready for a meeting is a massive undertaking, even if all you're trying to do is keep them quiet so you can have a mature conversation. At times, you will need to hire a babysitter in order to free you both to go to a fundraising event, but the cost of this can quickly add up if you multiply it by a few hundred meetings. For other meetings, you may be able to take the kids along, particularly if you are meeting with someone who has never met your children, and the location has an easy place for them to play while you talk (like the playground at

Chick-Fil-A). Many times, you should invite people over to your house so the kids can play in familiar surroundings or watch a movie while the adults talk. In short, you will have to be creative. Figure out which of the meetings need both the husband and wife to attend and map out a plan that fits each circumstance best.

BUT, WHAT ABOUT ALL THOSE MEETINGS?

If you are following the basic fund raising paradigm presented above, then you're probably asking this question. Yes, I'm arguing that you should work to have personalized meetings with each of your potential donors. For some of you, this may mean 150–200 meetings. If you can do 15 meetings a week, you will need 10–15 weeks to raise funds well, if you devote full-time attention to the task.

One approach can help you combine some of these meetings and may make for a more effective fundraising meetings on some occasions. This method should not be seen as an alternative to the aforementioned model or a way to speed up the process.

Look over your list of potential donors. While you may observe substantial diversity represented on the list, some of the individuals on the list likely know one another. Also, you may notice that certain people on the list could naturally connect you to many others on the list. For example, this may be a couple who has lived in a certain area for a long time and has led Bible studies or small groups, or who excels at hospitality. When these connectors throw a party, everyone shows up. You can leverage their relational capacity in your favor.

Ask the connecting couple if they would be willing to host a dessert or coffee at their house one weeknight and invite their friends to hang out together and learn more about the work you are doing. Ideally, you can suggest the names of five or six other couples whom they know and whom you believe would naturally accept an invitation to their home. Also, you should ask them to expand the invitation to any contacts they know and would like to invite, though limiting the group size to around 20 people is wise. You should offer to bring the desserts, coffee, and drinks, so that all they will need to do is invite the guests and open their home.

On the night of the party, you should show up and build casual relationships with the guests—some of whom you may know and some you may not. This time allows the guests to meet your spouse or children in a relaxed atmosphere.

After some time to mingle, gather the guests and make the same presentation you use in the one-on-one appointments. Pass out your vision page and share the plan for your work with everyone in attendance. Depending on your personality, you may find that this environment is a better context for you to share you vision. For example, I tend to excel in mid-to-large sized groups where content is shared in a more presentational fashion. Smaller settings, especially one-on-one dialogues over coffee, are far more difficult for me. The goal in the larger settings is the same—cast a compelling vision for your work and invite others to be involved. You should discuss the three primary ways they can be involved in your work and ask if they would consider praying, giving, or going, just as you would if you were talking to isolated individuals.

The process of commitment may also be easier using this model. Recall in the earlier stage I mentioned that awkwardness that may come from asking people to hand you a commitment card in the middle of a coffee meeting. They may need time to consider or to consult with a spouse, a task that is obviously difficult if they are sitting a booth next to you. But, a party offers plenty of space for this to happen. Once you finish making the presentation, invite the hearers to continue to fellowship over dessert and turn in a card in a basket on a table or by the front door before they leave. This time will allow them to talk briefly with their spouse and make their decisions.

BUT, WHAT ABOUT LARGER GROUPS?

The simple answer is that larger groups follow the same paradigm if you are talking to a small group, Bible study, or Sunday School class. These built-in groups cultivate a natural context to apply the above model.

If you are given a chance to present your ministry to an entire church, you can, once again, follow the same pattern with minor modifications. You will likely not have 45-minutes to make your presentation, so you will need to develop a 10-minute talk that walks through the details of your mission and the ways people can be involved. In most cases, church leaders will allow their members to reach out to you if they are interested in supporting your work. You can give out your contact information, and if someone contacts you, begin at the phone call stage in the one-on-one model and go from there. Other settings may allow you to have your commitment cards with you as you speak and give them to supporters who approach you after the service. In rare cases, pastors may allow you to put support cards on each seat and allow people to commit by turning them in during the invitation or after the service. If a pastor offers to take up a love offering on your behalf, you should always, and I mean always, turn it down! Well, no, not really. I was just checking to see if you were still reading carefully. Never turn down money. But, if given the choice, you should ask pastors to allow you to build an individual donor base rather than ask their members to give a one-time gift. Again, a $2,000 love offering is great, but you will be far better off walking out of the church with commitments from 20 individuals who agree to support you over the next three years.

One final word of warning is warranted. Do not, under any circumstances, make a financial appeal in a church gathering without the clear support and endorsement of the pastor. By this I mean more than simply the fact that the pastor is a good friend who has asked you to come and speak to his church. Rather, you must make it clear that you plan to ask people to give to support your work and make sure that he is willing to let you do so. Also, you must ask him exactly how he would like that giving handled (i.e. people approach you after the service, turn in cards in the offering plate, etc.). The consequences of failing to ask permission may be both embarrassing and costly. If he is unwilling to grant such a request, ask if the church would be willing to include your information in the next church newsletter or bulletin so those who want to support you can follow up.

BUT, WHAT ABOUT MONEY FROM CHURCH BUDGETS OR DENOMINATIONAL GROUPS?

Praise God for healthy churches and supporting denominations. These groups are often significant catalysts for the work of church planting and missions; however, rather than depending on these groups, a wise fundraiser sees them as a supplement to their already effective strategy for raising money from individual donors. Far too often, church planters put all their eggs in the church support basket only to learn that these baskets are inherently volatile. Churches over-promise and under-deliver, get behind on budget, or simply take months upon months to make funding decisions. You will be wise to diversify your approach and not depend on churches exclusively, but this does not mean that you should not depend on them at all.

If you have occasions to meet with pastors, deacon boards, or denominational leaders, approach them just as you would any other fundraising appointment. Schedule a meeting, dress professionally, and cast a compelling vision. There are a few unique factors to keep in mind. First, you are likely to get more questions about theology or ministry philosophy from these leaders. Be prepared to articulate clearly what you believe and why you are doing ministry the way you are. Second, recognize the presence of the elephant in the room. Pastors have likely been burned by a fellow staff member who carelessly went down the road and started a new church or have seen the shrapnel of young leaders who came in the city without a proper theological or missiological foundation and ended up doing more harm than good. Mission pastors have likely known many who have taken financial benefit from the church and didn't respond with gratitude. Every pastor faces all sorts of financial pressure and meaningful ministries that vie for his time and attention. Go ahead and acknowledge these wounds and posture yourself with humility from the outset. Even if the church is unwilling to support you, perhaps you can change his perception of young leaders. Whatever you do, avoid a condescending tone that communicates that you have finally figured out the secret to doing church perfectly. Such a posture invariably communicates that the church to whom you are speaking doesn't have it all together like your church surely will. Finally, make it a point to start these meetings at a time when churches are making financial decisions. To set up a meeting with a deacon board in February is unwise. The church has just approved a new budget and will not likely consider new requests until the following year.

CONCLUSION

While I'm certain the list of questions could go on and on, it's time to conclude. By this point, you should have a foundation in place for a successful fundraising journey. I write as one who not only loves the church and believes in this process, but also as one who has walked this road. Over three months in the summer of 2009 my wife and I raised full support for our family and a few friends to plant Renewal Church, a church that is thriving in the northern part of Greenville, South Carolina today. The fruit of our fundraising efforts is attributable to the kindness and grace of God and the method I've outlined in this book. A similar process has been used to send college missionaries through ministries like Cru and plant hundreds of healthy churches around the world, like our sending church, Crosspoint Church in Clemson, SC where I learned many of these skills. I pray that God would use it in your life as well as we all prayerfully seek to send laborers for the gospel throughout the world.

32969173R10041

Made in the USA
Middletown, DE
25 June 2016